Readings and itineraries
5

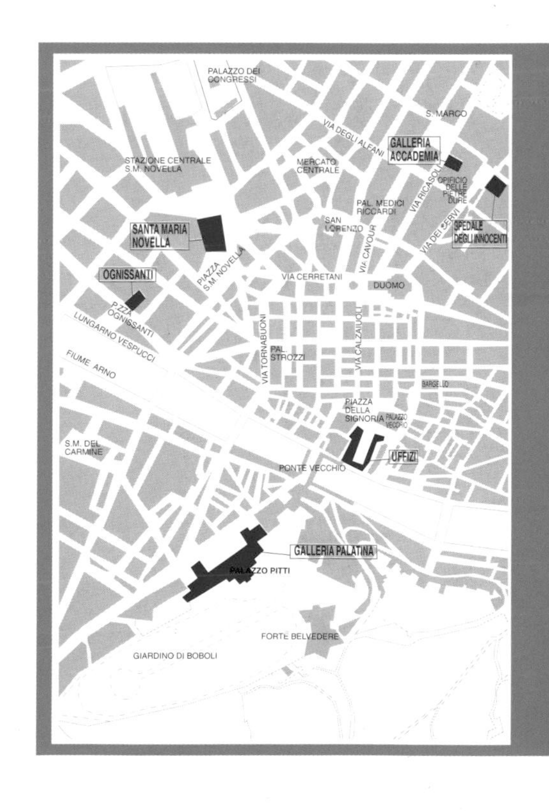

Other books in this series:
Raffaele Monti, *Piero della Francesca*
Raffaele Monti, *Leonardo da Vinci*
Cristina Acidini Luchinat, *Raphael*
Raffaele Monti, *Michelangelo Buonarroti*

On p. 30:
The Return of Judith (detail)
p. 31:
Adoration of the Magi (detail)
p. 32:
Primavera (detail)

A publication of
s i l l a b e s.r.l.
www.sillabe.it

managing editor: *Maddalena Paola Winspeare*
graphic design: *Laura Belforte*
editing: *Bettina Müller*
translation*: Antony Cafazzo*

reproduction rights: *Archivio SBAS*; *Archivio sillabe - foto: P. Nannoni, N. Orsi Battaglini, R. Bardazzi*
photolithography: *La Nuova Lito - Firenze*

ISBN 88-8347-072-9

Ilaria Taddei

Readings and itineraries

Botticelli

sillabe

Nowadays crowds perpetually flock to the Uffizi room given over to the works of Alessandro Filipepi, better known to the world as Botticelli. Yet the artist's two most admired works, those over which visitors linger most, *Primavera* and *The Birth of Venus*, were nearly unheard-of until the early 19th century. In fact, it was only in the middle decades of that century that the now renowned painter was rediscovered, thanks above all to English artists and art-lovers. Ever since, Sandro Botticelli has enjoyed incomparable popularity, unconditional admiration and tribute bordering on fetishism.

These two profane allegories reflect the refined climate of the 'court' of Lorenzo il Magnifico, for which the sensitive and receptive Botticelli was one of the greatest interpreters. However, this was before the history of Florence and Botticelli's artistic development were disrupted by the spiritual restlessness culminating in the tragic experience of Girolamo Savonarola.

Primavera, dated to about 1482, belonged to Lorenzo il Magnifico's cousin, Lorenzo di Pierfrancesco de' Medici, who kept it in his residences in Via Larga, near the famous palazzo that Cosimo the Elder had built. In the mid-16th century the work was found, together with *The Birth of Venus*, in the villa in Via Castello, where Giorgio Vasari saw it for the first time and in describing it was to establish the title by which it has been known ever since, *La Primavera (i.e., The Spring)*. The painting is an expression of the erudite cultural circle surrounding Lorenzo, which included the Neoplatonic philosopher, Marsilio Ficino, and the poet, Agnolo Poliziano, author of the *Le Stanze per la Giostra*. In fact, these are probably the literary references that, together with other classical works, would inspire Botticelli in his creating this masterpiece.

The painting must be read from left to right, beginning therefore with Zephyrus, the light spring wind who pursues the nymph Chloris and, in taking hold of her, endows her with the power to bear flowers (which in fact issue from her mouth), thereby transforming her into Flora, the Roman goddess of Spring. In the centre is Venus, and behind her, myrtle, her sacred plant; blindfolded Cupid wings above and darts an arrow in the direction of the Graces dancing in a circle. Finally, on the extreme left is the caduceus-bearing divine messenger, Mercury, intent on parting the clouds obscuring knowledge. In this reading therefore, the garden of Venus, symbol of *Humanitas*, hosts the passage of carnal love into spiritual and intellectual love. According to another interpretation, which also sees the work as representing Spring, the work was proba-

Opposite and following pages:

Primavera,
ca. 1482,
wood panel,
203 × 314 cm,
Florence, Uffizi.

Opposite and following pages:

The Birth of Venus, ca. 1484, canvas, 184.5 × 285.5 cm, Florence, Uffizi.

bly a wedding gift commissioned by Lorenzo il Magnifico for his cousin's marriage to Semiramide Appiani in 1482. The splendid garden is certainly a botanically faithful rendition of more than five hundred species of plants, many of which bloom between March and May in the hills overlooking Florence. The most recent hypothesis instead interprets it as an exaltation of the Liberal Arts, so that the figure in the centre would be, not Venus, but Philology. Therefore, it is all but clear what secret meaning is hidden behind this work, whose fascination lies in the languid elegance of its figures, rendered in bright colours thanks to Botticelli's use of oil temperas (that is, natural colours to which oils have been added). As models for the figures the artist used not only ancient sarcophagi, but coeval sculptural works, as well, such as the *David* by il Verrocchio for Mercury and, for Flora, Antonio del Pollaiolo's *Birth of the Baptist* on the silver altar of the Baptistery.
Equally linked to the cultured ambience of Laurentian Florence is the other, slightly earlier masterpiece, *The Birth of Venus* (circa 1484), cited by Vasari as found together with *Primavera* in the Castello Villa, once the country residence of Lorenzo di Pierfrancesco de' Medici. Although it is not known for sure whether this was the painting's original home, the fact that it was carried out on canvas, often used for profane themes destined for rural settings, does support this hypothesis. Once again, classical texts, such as Homer's *Hymn to Venus*, Ovid's love poetry, and Poliziano's verse were the likely literary reference that, together with classical figurative themes, such as the *Venus Pudica,* the painter drew inspiration from for this allegorical tale revolving around the goddess of beauty. Propelled over the waves on a floating shell by Zephyrus and Aura, the spring breezes laden with perfumes (alluded to by the roses), Venus lands ashore and is handed a flowered mantle by a young girl. The girl may represent one of the Hours, Venus' nymphs in waiting, or one of the Graces, charged with weaving the mantle of this goddess born of the fruitful union of Spirit with Idea, Matter with Nature.
In these works Botticelli, by now at the height of his craft, had already reached a well-measured, rational syntax through well-chosen formal elegance and colour transparency.
As Vasari narrates, after Botticelli's apprenticeship at a goldsmith's, where he acquired precision in sign and skill in the use of gold, his education was completed in the workshop of Filippo Lippi, where he began in 1464, thanks to the good offices of the Vespucci family who owned the house in Via Nuova, where Sandro lived with his family near the Church of Ognissanti.

Madonna and Child with angel, ca. 1465, wood panel,
95 × 65 cm,
Florence, Pinacoteca dello Spedale degli Innocenti.

Madonna and Child, young St. John and two angels, ca. 1468, wood panel,
85 × 64 cm, Florence, Gallery of the Accademia.

The 1465 *Madonna and Child with two angels* by Botticelli's maestro, Filippo Lippi, currently in the Uffizi, represents the model to which the budding student inspired for his early work on the same theme, currently in the Pinacoteca (Picture Gallery) of the Spedale degli Innocenti, though originally placed in a room adjoining the church sacristy of that institution, founded as a home for abandoned children. The theme of holy motherhood is therefore well suited to this first composition, in which Botticelli adds a number of highly innovative personal touches to his maestro's rendition: for instance, by replacing Lippi's open landscape background with an elegant arched window on textured-marble columns with bronze capitals. However, his otherwise strict conformity to his teacher's style allows dating this work to about 1465.
A later study on the theme of the Madonna and Child, in this case surrounded by young St. John and two angels, is the one now in the Gallery of the Accademia (though originally in the Ospedale di Santa Maria Nuova). Redolent of the style of Andrea del Verrocchio, this work can be dated to about 1468, after Lippi had already departed for Spoleto to complete his ultimate endeavour, the frescoes of the Cathedral apse, thus leaving Botticelli to study at Verrocchio's workshop for a time. His contact with Verrocchio,

Madonna and Child ("Madonna of the Rose Garden"), ca. 1470, wood panel, 124 × 65 cm, Florence, Uffizi.

Madonna and Child in Glory, ca. 1470, wood panel, 120 × 65 cm, Florence, Uffizi.

the 'all round' artist – at once, goldsmith, sculptor and painter – deepened his understanding of the relationship of figure with the space surrounding it, which he rendered through judicious use of lighting effects. The *"Madonna of the Rose Garden"* and the *Madonna and Child in Glory* came to the Uffizi in 1782 (however, without their original frames) due to the suppression of the Lorraine Chamber of Commerce. Their common frontal view of the full-length, seated figure shows how Botticelli had by now internalised Lippi's influence and incorporated Verrocchio's stylistics to achieve a wholly personal formulation, so much so that both works can be placed chronologically near the painter's first documented work, *Fortitude*, in 1470.

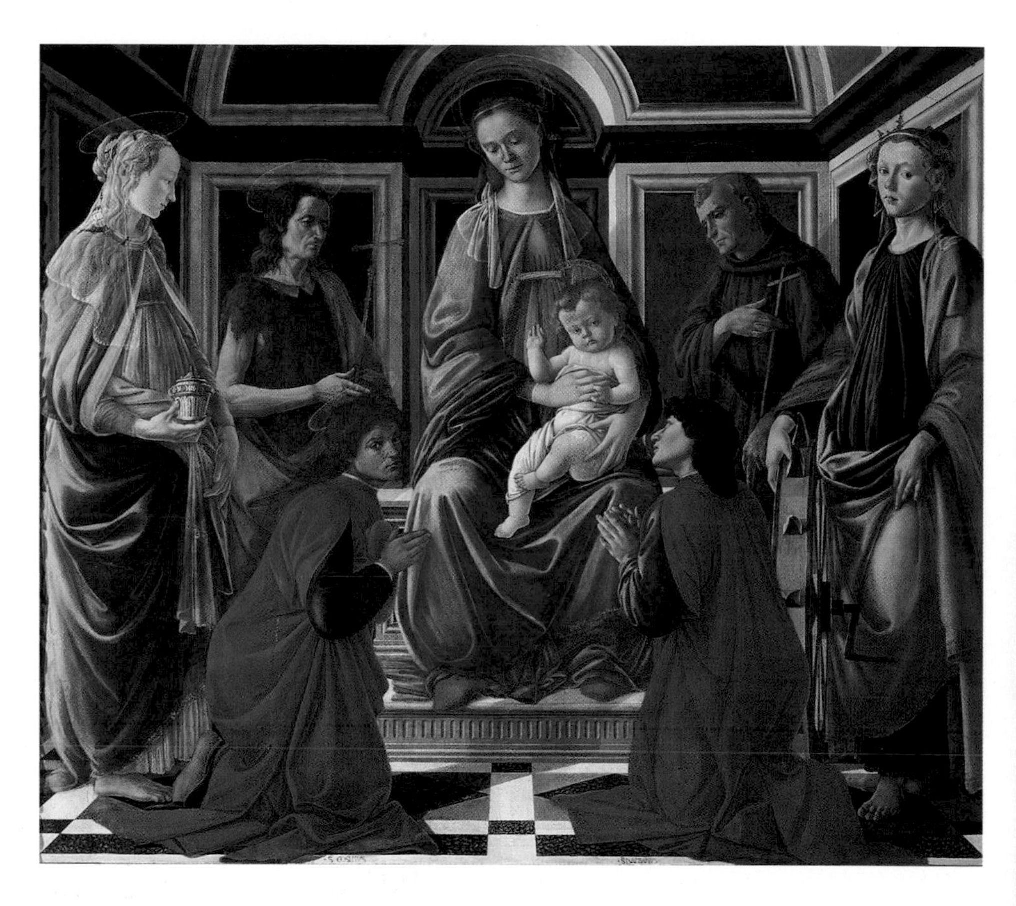

Madonna and Child with saints Mary Magdalene, John the Baptist, Francis, Catherine of Alexandria, Cosmas and Damian ("Altarpiece of Sant'Ambrogio"), 1467-1470, wood panel, 170 × 194 cm, Florence, Uffizi.

Just as the two Madonna's are strictly related, so *Fortitude* is to be considered in the same 'family' as the Saint Catherine depicted in the so-called *"Sant'Ambrogio Altarpiece"* (also in the Uffizi) though this latter is still permeated by Lippi's influence. Botticelli's first known great altarpiece (1467-1470), this *Madonna and Child with Saints*, came to the Uffizi from the Benedictine monastery of Sant'Ambrogio, although it was probably not carried out for that church. In fact, its original destination is still a matter of speculation, as the theory that identified it with the altarpiece of the Converted Sisters has by now been discarded, while it seems more probable that it was carried out for the high altar of the church of San Francesco in Montevarchi in the Valdarno. In an architectural layout punctuated by mosaics redolent of Leon Battista Alberti, the saints Mary Magdalene, John the Baptist, Francis and Catherine of Alexandria surround the throne of the Virgin and Child, while

Cosmas and Damian, the patron saints of the Medici family, kneel in the foreground.

Fortitude, 1470, wood panel, 167 × 87 cm, Florence, Uffizi.

Commissioned together with another of the Virtues, which was however never executed, *Fortitude* (1470) was meant to adorn the Sala delle Udienze (Hearing Room) of the Merchants Guild (located in piazza della Signoria) and thereby complete the cycle requested of Piero del Pollaiolo the previous year (perhaps because of a delay in its completion). Through Tommaso Soderini, consul of the Guild that year, this painting was to play a decisive role in Botticelli's career. The painter was introduced to Soderini (who was also the brother-in-law of Piero de' Medici, Lorenzo il Magnifico's father) by Giorgio Antonio Vespucci, Botticelli's neighbour as well as guardian of the consul's son. This provided Botticelli with the chance to prove his worth and enter the Medici entourage. *Fortitude* is seated on a heavily ornate polychrome stone and marble throne; the perspective is foreshortened from below. Her attributes are the studded club, in allusion to war, and the porphyry column, symbolising steadfastness. The silky soft, transparent dress adheres to her youthful body confined within glistening metal armour.

This same room of the Uffizi (no. 9) contains two wood panels with the Story of Judith and Holofernes, datable to 1470-1472. Originally, the two paintings constituted a diptych held within a carved and gilded frame (lost). Bianca Cappello, the second wife of grand duke Francesco I, received them as a gift from Rodolfo Sirigatti in 1584. They were later inherited by her son, Don Antonio, who kept them in his country manor in Via Larga. The compositions were clearly influenced by Antonio del Pollaiolo, particularly the facing for the altar of San Giovanni for the Baptistery, which is now in the Museo dell'Opera del Duomo. In the bright clear landscape of *The Return of Judith*, the biblical heroin advances haughtily and lightly, as if gliding over the ground, with her handmaiden, their dresses rippling in the wind. *The Discovery of the Body of Holophernes*, on the other hand, is distinguished by dramatic turmoil: in the confined space of a tent in the Assyrian camp, the light reveals the magnificent nude corpse of the beheaded Holofernes, surrounded by awe-stricken bystanders, almost as if in a macabre adoration of the Magi, in which pain and desperation accompany the wonderment.

The Return of Judith, 1470-1472, wood panel, 31 × 24 cm, Florence, Uffizi.

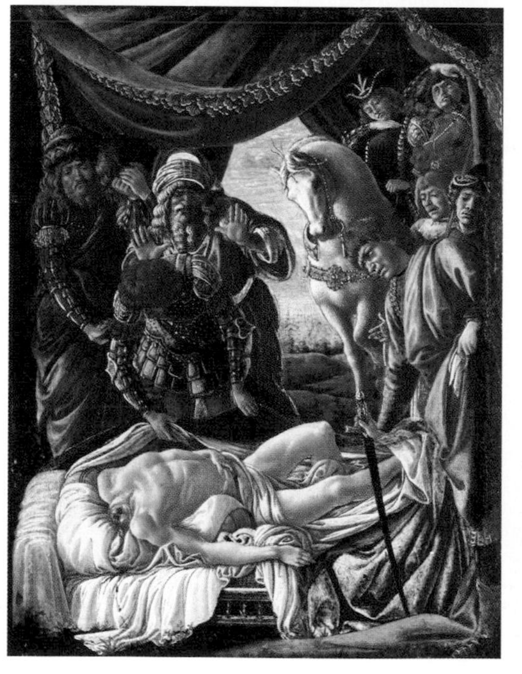

The Discovery of the Body of Holophernes, 1470-1472, wood panel, 31 × 25 cm, Florence, Uffizi.

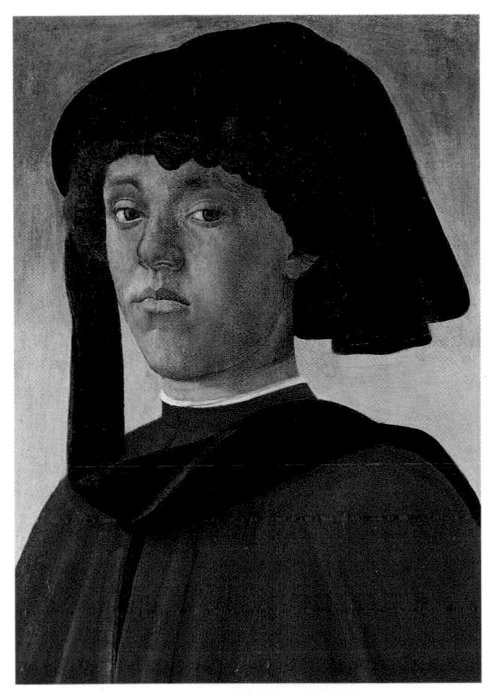

In these same years Botticelli tackled the genre of portraiture. The *Young Man Wearing a "Mazzocchio"* (ca. 1470) in the Prometheus room of the Palatine Gallery displays an imposing physical presence, despite some overzealous past cleansing that damaged the painting's surface. The youth is portrayed in a slightly rotated three-quarter pose, donning the typically Florentine *"mazzocchio"* headdress. The earlier work (certainly prior to 1475), *Portrait of a Young Man with Medal of Cosimo the Elder,* now in the Uffizi, contains a gilded plaster-cast medallion bearing the profile of Cosimo the Elder. The inscription: MAGNUS COSMUS MEDICES P(RIMUS) P(ATER) P(ATRIAE), refers to a title that was conferred him after his death in 1465. It is quite likely that the portrait itself depicts a medallist, identified by some art historians as Botticelli's brother, Antonio Filipepi, who was also a goldsmith for the Medici.

Portrait of a Young Man Wearing a "Mazzocchio",
ca. 1470, wood panel, 51 × 34 cm, Florence, Palatine Gallery.

Portrait of a Young Man with Medal of Cosimo the Elder,
1470-1475, wood panel and gilded plaster cast (medal), 56.5 × 44 cm, Florence, Uffizi.

Adoration of the Magi, ca. 1475, wood panel, 111 × 134 cm, Florence, Uffizi.

Nativity, ca. 1475, detached fresco, 200 × 300 cm, Florence, Santa Maria Novella.

Saint Augustine in his study, 1480, detached fresco, 152 × 112 cm, Florence, Church of Ognissanti.

The family resemblance can be appreciated in the *Adoration of the Magi,* in which Sandro portrays himself as the bystander with yellow mantle turned toward the spectator in the right foreground. This altarpiece, now displayed next to the portrait, was commissioned in about 1475 by Guasparre di Zanobi del Lama for the chapel at Saint Maria Novella of the Arte del Cambio, the powerful bankers' guild to which the Medici family also belonged. The subject, the Adoration of the Magi, was well in keeping with the chapel's title, dedicated to the Epiphany. However, it was also a theme very dear to the Medici family, who dressed as the oriental kings in the annual processions of the Company of the Magi. Thus, depicted in the panel are Cosimo the Elder, as the eldest king kneeling in front of Child Jesus, together with his two sons, Piero il Gottoso and Giovanni as the other two Magi. Also participating in this sacred event unfolding amongst ancient ruins are other members of the Medici house and their dearest friends: to the left, Giuliano, on whom Agnolo Poliziano is leaning, and next to them, Pico della Mirandola, while on the opposite side, is Lorenzo, dressed in red and black. Most likely the altarpiece was to be surmounted by the lunette frescoed with the *Nativity* that is now located above the main portal on the interior façade of Saint Maria Novella. Here, a contemplative St. Joseph stands amidst the ruins of a classical temple cell, recalling the *Adoration of the Magi*; Maria genuflects with fond attention toward the plump Child Jesus and vivacious (chromatically as

well) young St. John.

Still preserved today in the church of Ognissanti is *Saint Augustine in his Study*, a fresco that Botticelli executed in 1480 for the Vespucci family as the *pendant* to Domenico Ghirlandaio's *Saint Jerome*. Both were originally frescoed on the wall partition which once separated the choir areas from those given over to the faithful and then moved to their current locations by Vasari during restructuring of the ecclesiastical chambers. The heroic figure of St. Augustine, the Father of the Church, is rendered in a highly intense spiritual tone within his small study surrounded by the trappings of humanist knowledge: from the armillary sphere to Euclid's code. In the altar the painter makes reference to the elegance of Verrocchio's funeral monument to Piero and Giovanni de' Medici in the Old Sacristy of San Lorenzo.

Annunciation, 1481, detached fresco, 243 × 555 cm, Florence, Uffizi.

It was in the spring of the following year, 1481, that Botticelli carried out the fresco of the *Annunciation*, now in one of the rooms adjoining San Pier Scheraggio, the Romanesque church incorporated by Vasari into the Uffizi complex. It was originally found on a wall of the loggia of *Spedale di San Martino alla Scala*, a hospital where plague victims were cared for. The angel still hovers in the air with vestments flapping in the wind, while a compliant St. Mary awaits kneeling on a carpet in the opulent room marked by pillars with gilded capitals and elaborate shafts. While the perspective is reversed in the foreground scene, it extends to be lost in the depths of the landscape.
This is a happy time for Botticelli, during which he adheres to Neoplatonic doctrine, on the one hand, and to a more formal religious message, on the other. Clear testimony to the former comes from *Primavera*, *The Birth of Venus* and, still in the same room of the Uffizi, the canvas of *Pallas and the Centaur*. This last was painted around 1482, as usual for Lorenzo di Pierfrancesco de' Medici, and was found in the residences of the cadet branch of the family, in precisely the same ground-floor room as *Primavera*, which it followed in being transferred to Villa Castello. Even then, the available inventories did not agree on the identity of the young woman in the white dress emblazoned with the Medici ring with diamond and flowering branches under a green mantle. She carries a shield on her shoulder and an elaborately decorated poleaxe in her left hand, while the right holds the hair of a rather subdued-looking centaur armed with a longbow and full quiver of arrows. Over the years many interpretations have been proffered: in 1498 the two figures were described as Camilla with a satyr, then later, in 1516, as Pallas taming a centaur. Nowadays however, the philosophi-

Pallas and the Centaur, ca. 1482, canvas, 207 × 148 cm, Florence, Uffizi.

cal and moral reading prevails, by which, following the suggestions of Ficino, the conflict between reason and brute instincts waging in the twofold nature of the centaur (half man, half horse) can be reconciled thanks to the mediation of divine wisdom, personified by Pallas. According to this interpretation, the vines crowning her head and twining amongst her arms and breasts would be olive branches, the goddess' symbol. If instead, following the symbolism of *Psycomachia* by Aurelius Prudentius, the painting represents the struggle between Pride and Humility, then the branches would be from the myrtle plant traditionally associated with this virtue.

Madonna of the Magnificat, 1481-1485, wood panel, Ø 118 cm, Florence, Uffizi.

As for the religious message, Botticelli, in keeping with his profane works during the 1480s, translates it into rich, intellectually meditated painting enriched by a profusion of exquisite detail. He exhibited a penchant for *tondos* destined for private worship or the seats of the various *Arti* (i.e. Guilds), hence the genesis of masterpieces such as the *Madonna of the Magnificat* (1481-1485) and the *Madonna of the Pomegranate* (1487), both currently in the Uffizi. These are lucid visions, intentionally distorted as if by a mirror: the former (named for the opening lines of the Virgin's

Madonna of the Pomegranate, 1487, wood panel, Ø 143.5 cm, Florence, Uffizi.

Prayer visible in the open book in the painting) offers a convex optical perspective, while the latter is seen from a concave point of view. This latter is still in its original frame with golden lilies on a blue background, in all likelihood executed by Giuliano da Maiano and his workshop, who were also the authors of the similar design on the ceiling of the Sala dell'Udienza (Hearing Room) of Palazzo della Signoria. In fact, the painting was destined for the Tribunale dei Massai di Camera (Chamber Stewards' Court), located in that same building.

In about 1487, the Physicians' and Chemists' Guild commissioned from Botticelli the monumental altarpiece for the high altar of the church under its patronage, San Barnaba. Botticelli depicts the *Enthroned Madonna and Child with saints Catherine of Alexandria, Augustine, Barnabas, John the Baptist, Ignatius and Michael the Archangel*, today in the Uffizi. In the early 18th century this work was tampered with, and consequently the original frame and some stories on the predella were lost. The inscription on the throne's step, VERGINE MADRE FIGLIA DEL TUO FIGLIO (virgin mother daughter of your son) is the first verse of the last canto of Dante's *Paradise*; it testifies to Botticelli's profound knowledge of the poem regarding which he had done some sketches for the 1481 edition annotated by Cristoforo Landino.

Enthroned Madonna and Child with saints Catherine of Alexandria, Augustine, Barnabas, John the Baptist, Ignatius and Michael the Archangel ("St. Barnabas Altarpiece"), detail, ca. 1487, wood panel, 268 × 280 cm, Florence, Uffizi.

Coronation of the Virgin ("San Marco Altarpiece"), 1488-1490, wood panel, 375 × 256 cm, Florence, Uffizi.

The other great altarpiece, also in the Uffizi, bears witness to Botticelli's incipient spiritual and formal transformation. It was painted between 1488 and 1490 for the altar of the chapel of Saint Eligius, patron saint of goldsmiths, in the church of San Marco, patronised by the Arte della Seta (i.e., Silk Guild). Innovative in its composition, the *Coronation of the Virgin* presents a clear division of space: above, the Divine, with rejoicing angels immersed in golden radiance, and below, the Human, bearing the statuesque figures of the saints. John the Evangelist, patron saint of the Silk Guild, acts as intermediary between the two worlds, holding the as yet unwritten *Book of the Apocalypse*, while Augustine and Jerome, champions of the Marian mystery, meditate, and finally, Eligius, on the far right, beckons the viewer to contemplate the celestial vision above.

In 1489 the wealthy banker, Benedetto Guardi, commissioned the wood panel (now in the Uffizi) known as the *Cestello Annunciation,* destined for the altar of the family chapel in the church of the monks of the Cestello order in Borgo Pinti, now Santa Maria Maddalena de' Pazzi. Still in its original frame, the work represents the episode narrated in the Gospel according to Luke, as can be read in the predella, which also contains the coat of arms on its sides, and a dramatic, yet essential, Christ Figure in its centre. In the rigorous cubic space opening onto the landscape, the movements of the soul (angel and Virgin) are translated into dynamic poses enhanced by the jagged drapings embellished with filigreed borders – refinements worthy of a goldsmith. Suggestively, the figurative sources are two great works from the first half of the century, both datable to around 1440, Donatello's *Cavalcanti Annunciation* in Santa Croce and Filippo Lippi's panel of the same subject, now in the church of San Lorenzo.

Annunciation ("di Cestello"), 1489, wood panel, 150 × 156 cm, Florence, Uffizi.

ECCE · ANCILLA · DOMINI · FIAT
MICHI SECVNDVM VERBVM TVVM

Saint Augustine in his study, 1490-1495, wood panel, 41 × 27 cm, Florence, Uffizi.

Although characterised by refined formal elegance, Botticelli's final homage to the humanist culture is already permeated by the moral restlessness (incited by the vehement sermons of Fra Girolamo Savonarola) that were to mark the painter's late years (he dies in 1510). Ample testimony of Botticelli's state of mind is provided by the two small, yet precious panels in the Uffizi, *Saint Augustine in his study* and *Calumny*. According to some, the first, a devotional work painted in 1490-1495, was destined for two of Savonarola's acolytes, while others maintain it was for the prior of the Augustinian convent of Santo Spirito. The setting is a small niche decorated with ancient clypei and a bas-relief of the Madonna and Child in the lunette. The curtain is drawn to one side to impart movement to the scene and reveal the saint sitting and writing intently, as was his daily practice, as testified to by the paper fragments scattered throughout the floor. The other panel, executed in about 1494, is far more complex. The host of allego-

Calumny, ca. 1494, wood panel, 62 × 91 cm, Florence, Uffizi.

rical figures within a majestic hall reminiscent of Leon Battista Alberti prompts moral contemplation on Justice. Given by Botticelli himself to his banker friend, Antonio Segni, the work revisits the theme painted in the 4th century B.C. by Apelles, the apotheosis of Renaissance artists. The description of Apelle's painting, linked to the personal affairs of the painter accused of treason, was well-known at the time (through the 15th -century translations of the dialogue *De Calumnia* by Lucianus and Alberti's treatise on painting). Botticelli, therefore, offers an at once grandiloquent and miniaturist transcription of the work. The allegorical characters, Suspicion (back turned) and Ignorance, whisper in the king's donkey ears; immediately in front of them, Malice grasps the arm of Calumny, who is being primped by Envy and Deceit as she drags the naked, imploring victim by his hair. The procession is followed by black-robed Penitence, who turns toward naked Truth. This last figure, which in many ways, including its pose, corresponds to a classical Venus (except for her gesturing towards the sky) has by now lost all traces of sensuality, thereby underscoring how far Botticelli had come from his profane allegories of the 1480's.

Chronology

1445 Alessandro Filipepi, known as Sandro Botticelli, is born in Florence to Mariano, a leather tanner, and his wife Smeralda.

1464-1467 Works as apprentice in the workshop of Filippo Lippi and then Verrocchio.

1470 Paints *Fortitude*.

1472 Documented as a member of the Company of St. Luke, an association of artists.

1474 *Saint Sebastian* (now in Berlin) is placed in the Church of Santa Maria Maggiore in Florence on January 20. The same month he is invited to Pisa to execute frescoes in the cemetery, a project never carried out.

1475 Paints the standard of Giuliano de' Medici (now lost) for the Joust in Piazza Santa Croce.

1478 After the Pazzi conspiracy, he is commissioned to fresco effigies of the conspirators above the door of the customs office of Palazzo della Signoria; the project is cancelled in 1494, after the Medici flee Florence.

1480 Paints *Saint Augustine* for the church of Ognissanti.-

1481 Executes the *Annunciation* for San Martino alla Scala. On October 27, together with Cosimo Rosselli, Domenico Ghirlandaio and Perugino, signs the contract to fresco the walls of the Sistine Chapel in Rome; by February of the following year, has completed at least eleven popes, *Scenes from the Life of Moses*, the *Temptation of Christ* and *Punishment of Korah*.

1482 Returns from Rome and completes *Primavera* and *Pallas and the Centaur*.

1483 With others from his workshop, performs four panels with *The Story of Nastagio degli Onesti*, of which three are now in Madrid and another in a private collection.

1484 *The Birth of Venus*

1485 Is paid for the Bardi Altarpiece (originally in Santo Spirito, now in Berlin).

1487 Paints the *Madonna of the Pomegranate*.

1489 Executes the *Annunciation* for the Guardi chapel of the Cestello church.

1498 Paints the *Stories of Virginia and Lucrezia* for Guidantonio Vespucci (now held in Bergamo and Boston).

1501 Finishes the *Mystic Nativity* (now in London), his only signed and dated work.

1504 Takes part in the committee charged with deciding where to place Michelangelo's *David*.

1510 Dies on May 17 and is buried in the church of Ognissanti.

Bibliography

J. A. Crowe-G. B. Cavalcaselle, *A new history of painting in Italy from the second to the sixteenth century*, 3 voll., II, London 1864-1866, pp. 414-430.
H. Ulmann, *Sandro Botticelli*, München 1893.
I. B. Supino, *Sandro Botticelli*, Firenze 1900.
H.P. Horne, *Alessandro Filipepi, commonly called Sandro Botticelli, painter of Florence*, 2 voll., London 1908; ed. italiana a cura di C. Caneva con appendici inedite, Firenze 1987.
W. von Bode, *Botticelli*, Berlin 1921.
A. Schmarsow, *Sandro del Botticello*, Dresden 1923.
A. Venturi, *Botticelli*, Roma 1925.
Y. Yashiro, *Sandro Botticelli and the Florentine Renaissance*, London-Boston 1925.
C. Gamba, *Botticelli*, Milano 1936.
L. Venturi, *Botticelli*, Wien 1937.
J. Mesnil, *Botticelli*, Paris 1938.
S. Bettini, *Botticelli*, Bergamo 1942.
G. C. Argan, *Botticelli*, Genève 1957.
R. Salvini (a cura di), *Tutta la pittura del Botticelli*, 2 voll., Milano 1958.
L. D. e H. S. Ettlinger, *Sandro Botticelli*, London 1976.
R. Lightbown, *Sandro Botticelli Life and Work*, 2 voll., London 1978.
U. Baldini, *Botticelli*, Firenze 1988.
N. Pons, *Botticelli. Catalogo completo*, Milano 1989.
L. Vertova, *Divagazioni su Botticelli (vero e falso)*, in "Artista", I, 1989, pp. 98-109.
C. Caneva, *Botticelli. Catalogo completo*, Firenze 1990.
M. Levi D'Ancona, *Due quadri del Botticelli eseguiti per nascite in casa Medici. Nuova interpretazione della Primavera e della Nascita di Venere*, Firenze 1992.
E. Capretti, *Botticelli*, Firenze 1997.
F. Zöllner, *Botticelli Toskanischer Frühling*, München-New York 1998.
Sandro Botticelli. Dipinti e disegni per la Divina Commedia, catalogo della mostra (Roma), 2 voll., Milano 2000.

Printed in May 2001
by Media Print, Livorno,
for
sillabe